BYWAYS OF THE NORTHWEST

COVER PHOTO:

Shepperds Dell trail descends from the old Columbia River Highway beneath great domes of basalt into this small alcove where you may find the great wonders of the Gorge, in delicate ferns growing from clinging moss or in the gentle fold of the waterfall. To reach the old highway, now called the Scenic Route, from 80N take the Lewis and Clark State Park exit just east of Troutdale and across the Sandy River. You'll be heading south for a while, then swinging east, and you'll have a chance to stop at viewpoints, like Portland Womens Forum State Park and Crown Point, high above the Columbia and you can look far up and down the river and into Washington State. Traveling the byways is the fun of getting there.

I

BYWAYS OF THE NORTHWEST

BY R. MOLAND REYNOLDS

International Standard Book Number   0-912856-29-7
Library of Congress Catalog Number   76-662
Copyright 1976 by Graphic Arts Center Publishing Company
2000 N.W. Wilson • Portland, Oregon 97209   503/224-7777

Designer • Robert Reynolds
Printer • Graphic Arts Center
Bindery • Lincoln & Allen

Printed in the United States of America

These are pictures of the region in which we live. They show the remarkable diversity of the land, some of the changes created by forces of nature, others by the pressure of people. Deep channels cut ages ago are made dry or are hidden in man-made lakes, as rivers are controlled by dams. Great mountains have been thrown up from beneath the earth and worn down by wind and water or eaten into by goldmining dredges. Orchards blossom and wheat fields turn golden in volcanic soil and desolate lands and contorted formations have been created by once molten lava. Weathered homesteads and ghost towns are returning to the soil and towns are restored to Victorian elegance. Waves pound a changing shore, streams cascade down the face of cliffs and generations of waterfowl seek refuge in protected lakes. Wheel marks of covered wagons can be found in prairies and mountain meadows not far from motor roads. This is a great land and there is much to see.

Byways is a guide book and also a statement about our land. I have tried to keep the photographs simple, direct, so that nothing comes between the viewer and what is there to be seen—and felt. This is a beautiful land, a marvelous one and there is the temptation to dramatize or romanticize, but there is no need; there is enough wonder in the land if we only take the time to look. You may argue the choice of some of the byways and photographs—and that is good, because it means that you have been looking and finding your own moments of discovery. My response is that of the fisherman: you should see the ones that got away, or in this case, those that were thrown away, for they, too, are worth the viewing. This, then, is a sharing of experience, and an invitation for you to seek out the quiet excitement and exhilaration of the many byways of the Northwest.

Victorian-era Flavel House, at 8th and Duane Streets in Astoria, now serves as the Clatsop County Historical Museum and displays a fine selection of regional artifacts. Astoria is northwest of Portland on Highway 30, which offers some interesting detours, but traveling the backroads through Mist and Jewell is a pleasure not to miss.

Garibaldi is a small community on the north shore of Tillamook Bay, where the wharf always has a great assortment of weather-beaten craft and salty sailors. To get there, follow Highway 101 eleven miles north of Tillamook (Jct. 101-6).

The little white Natal Schoolhouse is located on Highway 47 about three miles east of Mist. The one-room building is similar to many turn-of-the-century rural schoolhouses.

Waysides along Highway 101, beginning two miles north of Neahkahnie, offer exhilarating vistas of the Oregon coastline. The road opposite the golf course leads to the trail up Neahkahnie Mountain, which rises 1795 feet above the ocean and the sands which are said to hold buried treasures from Spanish galleons.

Yaquina Head lighthouse, built in 1871, stands high above the Pacific. A wonderful, and sometimes windy, viewpoint from which to look down on the beaches, and far out to ocean freighters, deep sea fishing boats and whales. Off coast Highway 101 at Agate Beach, two miles north of Newport.

Lake Creek shoots over a series of enormous, smooth rocks in a section of falls known locally as "slippery rocks". During summer months when waters are lower, folks come here for an afternoon of rocksliding. The creek is located southwest of Triangle Lake on Highway 36.

This unique round barn, constructed of concrete walls and a tin roof is located three miles northeast of Triangle Lake along a beautiful stretch of Highway 36. The highway meanders through the Coast Range until it joins Highway 126 near Florence.

Follow Highway 101 north of Newport to Agate Beach and take the lighthouse road out to the tip of Yaquina Head. Grassy knolls drop abruptly into the ocean; below are huge rocks and a beautiful little beach of smooth black stones.

Yachats, pronounced Ya-hots, which the Indians say means "at the foot of the mountain", is the name of the town and of the river which flows into the ocean here. There is easy access to the rugged coastline, where you can walk along the rocks, study delicate sea life in tidal pools and sometimes, dodge the spray from waves and of sea spouts bursting up from small blowholes.

Morning fog at Winchester Bay can create ghostly silhouettes, but you can hear the voices of fishermen, the rattling of boat rigging and the screams of hungry gulls. A popular salmon and crab-fishing harbor. Along Highway 101, four miles south of Junction 38 at Reedsport.

The Coast Guard Boathouse at Garibaldi, is both an elegant and utilitarian structure, and the narrow walkway and supporting poles create varied and interesting patterns over the bay. The road to the boathouse is off Highway 101, directly south of the Coast Guard Station at the west side of town.

Sand dunes create a golden desert from Florence to Winchester Bay and beyond. A climb to the top of the dunes will give you a workout, but will also offer you an exciting new world of skeletal trees, pine-covered knolls and small blue lakes. South Jetty Road off Highway 101, one-half mile south of Florence will take you to the dunes, beach and the jetty at the mouth of the Siuslaw River.

Jacksonville, born during the southern Oregon gold rush of the 1850's survived as the mercantile center for the surrounding farm community. The railroad by-passed the town for the then tiny Medford in 1883, and Jacksonville remained isolated. Buildings and homes have been impressively restored to nineteenth century frontier elegance; the museum is fascinating. Jacksonville is west of Medford on Highway 238.

You may reach McKee Bridge by traveling west from Jacksonville to Ruch on Highway 238, then south eight miles on Applegate Road. Picnic grounds here are thickly shaded and the Applegate is a delightful little river in which to cool your feet after walking the streets of Jacksonville. The covered bridge is open only to foot traffic.

Brownsville, an early woolen mills town, situated on the Calapooya River, is four miles east of I-5 on Highway 228. Buildings of the business district have retained the false fronts of pioneer days; among them is the Linn County Historical Museum. South of the business district is the J. M. Moyer house built in 1881.

Highway 38 runs alongside the Umpqua River through the Coast Range. During late summer there are some fine blackberry pickings here, and occasionally, a small craft sputters its way upstream.

The Indians called the butte southeast of the town of Mount Angel, *Tap-a-lam-a-ho*, a place of communion with the Great Spirit. Now it is the site of a Benedictine abbey and seminary where you may walk the beautiful grounds and enjoy the vista of the surrounding farmlands. Among the structures here is an outstanding contemporary library designed by Finnish architect Alvar Aalto. At Woodburn, take Highway 214 east to reach the town of Mount Angel; bean fields and hop fields are among the sights along the way.

An oak tree stands isolated in wheatland south of Amity. During spring and summer great patches of oak shield farm yards from the weather and from view. During fall and winter months, you can see the pioneer barns and homesteads usually hidden by foliage.

For a quiet interlude during an afternoon drive, take a free ride across the Willamette River on the electric-powered Canby ferry, *M. J. Lee*. Access is two miles north of Canby on North Holly Street (Old Ferry Road).

The oldest Catholic church in the state is at St. Paul, south of Newberg on Highway 219. Built in 1846, it replaced the original log church on French Prairie, where Archbishop Blanchet established St. Paul Mission in 1839. The red bricks were baked in kilns on the church grounds.

South of Amity along Highway 99W you have access to many delightful country roads leading through the valley farm lands. These are roads worth getting lost on and enjoying the oak trees, weathered barns and gently sloping fields.

One city block off Highway 99E in Aurora, you will find the intriguing
Ox Barn Museum with its fine collection of early American and Aurora-
colony artifacts. You can reach it by traveling east from Interstate 5 or
south from Oregon City on Highway 99.

You can picnic in the shade of oak and maple trees and enjoy the 150 varieties of fruit trees in the pioneer orchard. Bybee-Howell House was built in 1856 and has been restored by the Oregon Historical Society. Off Highway 30, ten miles north of Portland, the first right turn along Sauvie Island Road leads to the house.

Sauvie Island game management areas are a delight to the senses: the marsh has a thick earthy odor; the bright colors of the male mallard contrast with the patterned brown of the hen; birds nesting in the area respond to the call of others in flight; and if a twig snaps underfoot, there's an explosion of sound as birds beat their way into the air. The management areas have been set aside for the protection of wintering waterfowl, but are open to everyone. Just ten miles from Portland out Highway 30, less than that from the industrial area, and you are in a world apart.

Tanner Creek waterfall, just around the bend as you start up the forest path, which you reach by taking the Bonneville exit off Interstate 80N and traveling south about two hundred yards on the gravel road.

Larch Mountain road winds fourteen miles through lush Cascade forest to the summit, 4045 feet above sea level. On a clear day, you can see towering snow-capped peaks in both Oregon and Washington.

Horsetail Falls is about six miles east of Bridal Veil exit off Interstate 80N, but the unhurried route is taking the Lewis and Clark State Park exit and following the Scenic Highway. From Horsetail Falls, you can take a mile-and-a-half hike over Oneonta Gorge along a forest trail and return to the highway a half-mile to the west of the falls.

Columbia River sturgeon resting in a pool at Bonneville Fish Hatchery, almost like prehistoric monsters with their skeletal structure on the outside, are known to survive up to one hundred fifty years. You can visit the many areas of the hatchery where millions of salmon and trout are raised from eggs to the size at which they are released into tributaries of the Columbia River. Display cases in the main building show the many fresh-water and salt-water species found around Oregon. At some of the outdoor pools you can buy food pellets to feed the larger fish and watch as they churn the water fighting to get their share.

A marsh lake on the Columbia, a quarter-mile east of Horsetail Falls on the scenic route, reflects the Washington mountains across the river. It is a lake only during the rainy seasons; in summer it is a field of golden grass.

Cloud Cap Inn, at the summit of Cooper Spur, was built by architect William H. Whidden for his Portland clients, William Ladd and Charles Wood. The inn opened in 1899 and for many years served as base camp for mountaineers scaling the treacherous north face of Mount Hood. Follow Highway 35 south from Hood River, through Cooper Spur and up the gravel service road S-12.

Homestead near Wasco shows the wear from wind and sun of the upland country. There is much to see along Highway 206, from weather-beaten reminders of the pioneers to isolated farm houses surrounded by vast wheat fields.

Locust Grove Church stands almost hidden from the highway, a quiet reminder of earlier days. Built in the 1890's, it now is used to store feed. Highway 206, seven miles beyond The Dalles on Interstate 80N at the Celilo exit, runs southeast, towards Wasco, through rugged farm and cattle land.

Grass Valley, south of Biggs Junction twenty-eight miles on Highway 97, was named by pioneers who would tell greenhorns that rye grass in this part of the country grew higher than a man's head, and if this brought no response, they would add "when he's on horseback." An abandoned church, overtaken by long grass and trees, rests near the center of town. The thick walls and sturdy wood construction of the nearby grain elevator are worth viewing.

Mosier Loop, five miles east of Hood River off Interstate 80N, meanders for nine beautiful miles through cherry orchards and cattle country; it peaks at Rowena Crest Viewpoint and winds down to Rowena and 80N. The countryside here is a dramatic change from dense, evergreen west Cascades.

Mill Creek Gorge is a deep gash through the flat, open sage and juniper lands east of the Cascades. Highway 26 descends from Government Camp through forests of tall fir and pine into arid expanses with a scattering of juniper.

Shaniko boomed from obscurity at the turn of the century into a thriving shipping center for the great sheep herds of Central Oregon. Prosperity dwindled after a decade, when another railroad was built to the west. Now, you walk down boardwalks, which go nowhere in particular, and see fine old structures that have withstood the elements. There's an interesting collection of oldtime wagons and buggies and the old hotel is a museum in itself. Drive fifty-seven miles south of Biggs Junction on Highway 97.

Sherars Falls, where the waters of the Deschutes drop and boil through a narrow channel of basalt, and where the Warm Springs Indians fish from rickety wooden platforms, reaching out into the turbulent river with their long-handled nets for the elusive steelhead. Eight miles east of Tygh Valley on Highway 216.

Deschutes waters take a violent dip before crashing over Sherars Falls, named for proprietor of the pioneer toll bridge and stage stop, Joseph Sherar. There are no longer any remains of the structures nor are there the exorbitant toll fees which the pioneers had to pay. Find the falls east of Tygh Valley on Highway 216.

Ten miles south of Kimberly on Highway 19 is the access road to the Thomas Condon Fossil Beds, named for the first geologist of the region. Formations of reworked volcanic ash have preserved evidence of a sub-tropical jungle with such fauna as sabertooth tigers, miniature horses and early bird species.

The John Day River meanders through existing rock formations of Picture Gorge and dry cattleland to the north. Islands of white stone lie stark amidst the dark green waters and teasel abounds along its banks.

Viewed from a higher elevation the Painted Hills look as if they were built of mounds of colored material with the shades of yellows, reds and even greens splashed on, and beginning to blend. From Prineville you go east on Highway 26 through Ochoco National Forest to reach the turn-off for Painted Hills State Park. This area around Prineville is the rock-hounds happy hunting ground for thunder eggs and agates.

You can follow the John Day River through seven counties from the Columbia through the Central Oregon plateau and find something new—or old—all along the way. This old barn and hay wagon were in an open field on Highway 19, east of the junction with Highway 207.

Barn, pond and split-rail fence lend a pastoral quality in this rugged sage country just east of the Cascade Range. Follow Highway 216 east of Junction 26 and explore the backroads through Wamic, Shaniko and Antelope, or the whitewater of the Deschutes as it spills through rocks at Sherars Falls.

A house stands weather-battered in the countryside west of Antelope. The little town, situated in Antelope Valley was a stagecoach stop in the 1860's and grew into a rowdy supply center for ranch hands in the late eighteen hundreds. In 1898 the waterless town went up in flames; it was partially rebuilt, but died with the emergence of the Shaniko RR Station. Antelope is south of Shaniko on Highway 218.

Small homesteaders tilled the dry lands of the Northwest for short periods, but most gave way to the large ranches. Skeletons of the homesteading past remain in the open fields.

Just west of Tygh Valley is the town of Wamic, which was once the eastern entrance to the old Barlow Toll Road (which now makes a rugged byway through the mountains to Barlow Pass). On the road leading to the pioneer Smock Prairie School, you can see a magnificent split-rail fence and Lone Pine cemetery splashed with brightly colored wildflowers. In some sections of the prairie you can still see the wheel ruts of the covered wagons.

The Smith Rock formation appears to have surged from the earth, as it looms ominously above Crooked River. There are trails to the base of the rock towers and you can follow the river through yellow-red canyons. Smith Rock Park is three miles east of Highway 97 at Terrebonne.

There's a highway west of Madras which heads south along Lake Billy Chinook to Cove Palisades Park, and to a dirt road leading to Sisters. You travel through the juniper and sage of the high country and into the pine forests. West and south of Sisters you can see the snow-capped peaks of Mount Washington, the Three Sisters and Broken Top.

Collier Memorial State Park, about 30 miles north of Klamath Falls on Highway 97, features a museum of logging equipment from the days of oxen and horse-drawn gear and steam-powered rigs. Some of the wheels were built to straddle huge logs. Youngsters enjoy crawling about the equipment and climbing up to the operator's platform.

Union Creek is a wayside just west of Crater Lake National Park on Highway 62. A short road north of town leads to an excellent vantage point to view the Rogue River as it plunges into a narrow rock gorge. From this point, a trail follows the river to Natural Bridge

At Natural Bridge, the turbulent Rogue disappears beneath a short rock platform, then emerges through a network of tunnels down river. Atop the rock, bubbles seep to the surface, and you can feel the power of the river churning beneath. These hidden channels were caused by the lava flow from the eruptions of Mount Mazama, which now holds the blue waters of Crater Lake. Natural Bridge Campground is west of Crater Lake National Park along Highway 62.

P Ranch was headquarters of the Peter French cattle empire before the turn of the century. His vast landholdings now belong to the Malheur Wildlife Reserve, where some 220 species of birds have been counted. Reminders of French's era are seen in the abundance of poplars, the remaining chimney of the white house, the weathered Long Barn and beef wheel. Follow Highway 205 south from Burns to Frenchglen; then go east on Steens Mt. Road one mile.

Frenchglen, about fifty miles south of Burns on Highway 205, is named for cattle baron Peter French and his father-in-law, Dr. Glenn. Horns and antlers attached to the side of a shed at the old hotel are weathered reminders of hunts in the Blitzen Valley region. This is a rich area for observing wildlife.

This round barn, designed by Pete French for winter horse-breaking, is built of rock masonry, rugged juniper posts and boards hauled over 100 miles. Drive Highway 78 southeast from Burns to Princeton and follow the red gravel road of the Malheur Reserve fourteen miles to the barn.

Surrounded by the Malheur National Forest is a long, flat valley floor, rich in grazing grasses. Highway 395 from John Day to Burns is an enjoyable stretch of road, abundant with wildlife and ever-changing landscapes from wilderness to desert.

Steens Mountain Road slowly rises above the Blitzen Valley and you aren't aware that you are on the summit until you look out at the phenomenal view. The eroded cliffs of the east side hold snow packs the year around. Follow Highway 205 south from Burns to Frenchglen, then take Steens Mountain Road east. The gravel road is well-maintained, but the weather is unpredictable during late fall and winter months.

An old jail and a few cabins like this one are all that remain of the town of Greenhorn, named during the 1860's gold mining days in the Blue Mountains. Follow Highway 26 east from John Day; shortly beyond mile-high Dixie Pass, turn north on the gravel road towards Sumpter, and then travel west on the road marked Greenhorn.

Sumpter still has a few hillside houses and huge gold-mining dredge standing as reminders of the boom days at the turn of the century. Most of the town was destroyed by fire in 1917. A twenty-mile drive along Powder River and into the Wallowa Whitman Forest, west on Highway 220 from Highway 7.

Whitney thrived as a sawmill and trading center during gold-fever days, though it never grew to more than two hundred people. A small-gauge railway came through but the tracks were pulled up when the boom fizzled. Follow Highway 26 east from John Day and take the gravel road marked Sumpter beyond Dixie Pass. Whitney is approximately twelve miles north of the turn-off.

Granite is on one of the many gravel and dirt roads which lead from Sumpter to ghost towns of the gold mining days in the Blue Mountains. A tavern, mercantile, school house and small graveyard are reminders of its boom town days. Highway 220 south of Baker will take you to Sumpter and a gravel road will lead you the remaining thirteen miles to Granite.

Gravel roads criss-cross a valley of dairy and cattle farms. To the west of Trout Lake, in Gifford Pinchot National Forest, you can hike Huckleberry Mountain (Big or Little), travel the Cascade Crest Trail, explore lava beds or ice caves (you should wear a helmet and carry a lantern). To the north is Mount Adams. Follow Highway 141 north from Bingen on the Columbia River.

Five miles north of White Salmon along Highway 141 on the way to Trout Lake, the green waters of the White Salmon River descend through the town of Husum and merge with Rattlesnake Creek.

Petroglyphs and pictographs of the ancient Indians are found in many areas of Washington, usually near streams, lakes and springs. These are on rocks near the Columbia, close to Horsethief State Park. From The Dalles Toll Bridge, follow Highway 197 to Highway 14. Drive through the park to the boat launch, and walk a short distance west along the railroad tracks to the petroglyphs.

East of Bingen on Highway 14 is a fascinating change of earth formations. Great slabs of barren rock slant into the Columbia, and huge billowy hill-sides create fantastic contrasts. Cattle and horses graze the short basalt plateaus along the highway.

Maryhill Museum is situated high above the Columbia in the arid central hills. The mansion was originally to be road-builder Samuel Hill's home, but following WW I he decided to make it a museum of his collections. Among other displays, the museum houses a fine assemblage of Indian artifacts and a room of sculptures by Rodin. Follow Highway 14 east from The Dalles Bridge, or travel south from Goldendale on Highway 97. (Cattle raised on the encompassing seven-thousand acres support the museum).

The force of the ancient Columbia can be seen in the steep-walled canyons it cut through mountains and the thick lava layers of the Columbia Plateau. Today, that power can be seen in the cascades that pour over the huge dams. This stretch of the river is near Pasco as it bends north into central Washington.

Middle Waitsburg Road rolls through the rich wheatlands of the Palouse country. Winds carried volcanic dust from the eruptions of Mount St. Helens, Hood, Adams and Rainier to enrich the soil. Northeast of Walla Walla (Indian for "many waters") by Highway 12.

Asotin, south of Clarkston on Highway 129; a sedate community on the Snake River. The highway continues south through the Grande Ronde River Gorge, on possibly, the windingest road in the state. The viewpoints from the highway and waysides are magnificent and well worth the long ride.

Palouse Falls was caused by massive Ice Age glacial flooding which altered the course of the Palouse River and caused it to rip through the lands with a series of water falls. The only remaining waterfall drops 200 feet into a basin, then down a deep gorge into the Snake River. Highway 260 south from Washtucna then east on 261.

At Steptoe Butte State Park, a narrow road encircles the butte as it climbs to the summit affording near-aerial views of Palouse lands. Gentle mounds of the Palouse country range from Spokane south to the Snake River. Follow Highway 271 to Oaksdale, then proceed south eight miles.

Due to the number of dams, the Columbia River appears as a series of great, docile lakes; the largest is the backwaters of the Grand Coulee Dam, Lake Roosevelt. "Miss Columbia" was one of several free ferries traversing the Lake Roosevelt waters, but now remains dry-docked along Highway 25, near Gifford.

The Bowl and Pitcher formation, at Riverside State Park northeast of Spokane on Highway 291, is an example of pillow basalt resulting from molten lava solidifying in water. There are several paths and a suspension bridge which provide different vantage points for exploring the rocks.

On Highway 25, north of Fort Spokane, is the distinctive bell steeple of a church in the town of Hunter. Highway 25, from Davenport to the Canadian border, is a tranquil drive through rolling wheat hills above the Columbia River.

North of Fort Spokane State Park, along Highway 25, is a magnificent barn in a gentle valley of wheat. The fort was situated at the mergence of the Spokane and Columbia Rivers, but only a single structure remains. A small brick museum offers an account of the fort's history through push-button recordings and a few artifacts.

The Dry Falls Wayside and Interpretive Center is two miles south of Highway 2, on Highway 17. During the last Ice Age, tremendous amounts of water spilled over the plateau and carved a network of gashes in the land, called "Channeled Scablands". The most impressive channel was through the Grand Coulee and over Dry Falls, which had a magnitude forty times greater than that of Niagara Falls.

In the southern section of the Okanogan Highlands the Methow River flows through apple orchard country not far from the cattle lands where the motion picture *The Virginian* was filmed. Many privately-owned suspension bridges cross the river near the town of Methow. Highway 153 runs in a northwesterly direction from its junction with Highway 97 north of Lake Chelan and connects with Highway 20 west of Okanogan.

The "Golden Medical Discovery" barn may be found at the west end of Waterville along Highway 2. Waterville rests at the edge of Big Bend wheat country; a few miles west the land drops down into the orchard land of Wenatchee (Indian for "place of the rainbow").

Sixteen miles northwest of Wenatchee, on Highway 2/97, take the Dryden exit. North Dryden Road, from the city center, traverses orchards high above the Wenatchee River, leads to some fine viewpoints and eventually returns to Highway 2/97 near Cashmere.

North Cascades Highway 20, encircled by rugged snow-capped peaks and enormous Douglas fir, is one of the finest scenic drives in the Northwest.

One-quarter mile east of Newhalem on North Cascades Highway 20 are reminders of an awesome turbulence. Because of the construction of power dams, water has been detoured around this section of riverbed, but immense boulders and pools hollowed out of rock remain as signs of the power of the Skagit River.

From Whidbey Island Keystone ferry-landing, follow Engle Road two miles to the Scenic Highway (Hill Road). This road takes you through tidy farmlands and a tunnel of battered fir above the Strait of Juan de Fuca. You may sit in high grass above the strait or wander the beaches below. The scenic drive joins Highway 20 in Coupeville.

Whidbey Island is the largest of the San Juan group and was named for Joseph Whidbey, who discovered it in 1792. It offers a variety of scenic and historic sites. There are ferries from Mukilteo and Port Townsend.

Mukilteo is a quiet town centered around its ferry to the southern tip of Whidbey Island. At the landing there is a cluster of small Coast Guard buildings, which are open to the public on weekends. West of Everett on Highway 526 off Interstate 5.

Lopez Island is principally agricultural with weather-beaten barns amid the golden wheatfields which slope gently to the deep green waters. The island caters little to the vacationer, but one may find maps with local sites at the island service stations and stores. Lopez Island is the first stop for the ferry from Anacortes. (The old barn is at the corner of Center and Cross Roads).

Fort Casey artillery post was established in the 1890's to protect key Puget Sound harbors. Old bunkers as well as regional historical exhibits in the Admiralty Point Lighthouse are open to the public, (the lighthouse is open April 1 through September 30). Take the Mukilteo Ferry to Whidbey Island and travel Highway 525 north to Keystone; from here, take Engle Road one-half mile to Fort Casey State Park.

La Conner reclines along the Swinomish Channel with elegant old buildings and a diversity of vessels. On the hillside in back of town is the Skagit County Historical Museum which gives a colorful account of local history. Drive west five miles from Anacortes–Whidbey Island exit off I-5 on Highway 20, then four miles south to La Conner.

Close to a mile beyond the Shaw Island ferry landing, on Blind Bay Road, you come to a rustic log cabin which houses the Historical Society and Library. Across the way is a tiny red schoolhouse and beyond, a quiet little pond; all are uniquely miniature and well-maintained, in what seems to be the Shaw Island way.

Shaw Island is the number two stop for the ferry from Anacortes. A quarter mile from the landing are a great number of weathered and decaying reef net boats, strewn over a private field. Reef net boats have been used for fishing throughout the San Juans since early settlement times. (The boats perform in pairs with forty to fifty-foot nets stretched between. Small ladders were built on some boats enabling the fishermen to climb up to observe and judge the best time to "pull" their nets.)

Blaine is on I-5 at Washington's northern border. The International Peace Arch is centered in a park maintained jointly by the United States and Canada. This area is considered international territory, and may be used freely by citizens of both countries without the formality of custom's inspection. South of the town on Bell Road is the quiet mouth of Dakota Creek.

The pastoral beauty of rich green fields and classic old barns are the lure of the Skagit Valley. Sam Calhoun, canoeing the Skagit Delta in 1864, chose to dike and farm the land; his prime vegetables brought the eventual diking of the entire valley. (The barn is north of Silvana near the Interstate 5 exit).

Walking is the best way to see Port Townsend. You can take the time to view the old brick and carpenter gothic homes and buildings and study the elegant details at close hand. And you can go down to the harbor to see the boats and watch the ferry come in. Information for your walking tour is available at the county museum on Water and Madison Streets. The museum is a great place to visit, not only for the historical artifacts but also for information about the town's lively background.

Deception Pass is a deep tidal chasm between Whidbey and Fidalgo Islands crossed by two bridges one hundred eighty feet high. From the wayside or bridges there's a spectacular view, especially during incoming tides when waves stand on end as they force their way through the narrow corridor of the pass. You can reach Deception Pass from the south by ferries from Mukilteo or Port Townsend which lead to Highway 20 on Whidbey Island or off Interstate 5 near Mt. Vernon to Highway 20 and Fidalgo Island.

Between the Elwha River and the access road to Olympic National Park is a beautiful moss-covered woods. The park has an area of over eight hundred thousand acres and there are many roads and trails into the region. The rugged peaks of the Olympic Mountains, with year-round glaciers and snowfield, tower over the magnificent forests. There are mountain meadows, lakes and waterfalls, and the streams are excellent for trout. There are countless species of birds and animals, including Roosevelt elk, deer and bear. West of Port Angeles on Highway 101.

The Elwha entrance to the Olympic National Park may be reached by following Highway 101 east of Port Angeles to the Elwha River. The road hugs the river for several miles, then climbs high into the Olympics.

When you drive Highway 112 from Port Angeles to Neah Bay, you will see many rocks, like these near Sekiu, that show the battering of the sea. On the way you will go through the town of Pysht, which means "river of fish." The highway is heavily eroded and repairs seem to be continual. The strip of land across the Strait of Juan de Fuca is Vancouver Island, British Columbia.

Cape Flattery is situated at the far northwestern tip of the Olympic Peninsula on the Makah Indian Reservation. A gravel road from Neah Bay takes you to the short, generally muddy foothpath, and out over tremendous eroded cliffs and coves of the cape. Take the 112 cut-off, west of Port Angeles, from Highway 101 and follow it to its end. Offshore is Tatoosh Island, site of lighthouse operations since 1857.

Wesport is all about salmon fishing, but offers some pleasant alternatives. You can drive out the narrow south jetty, wander sand dunes, or poke through the boat-yards. Westport is on Highway 105, west of Aberdeen.

Some beautiful grasslands bordering Willapa Bay. Highway 105 west from Raymond will take you around the northern end of the bay to ocean beach towns and north to Grays Harbor. An interesting byway is to the community of Tokeland, named for Chief Toke of the Willapa Tribe.

Long Beach Peninsula, an accumulation of sediment spewed by the Columbia River, reaches northward slowly enveloping Willapa Bay. Its northern extremity, Leadbetter Point, is a windy sea-battered wildlife reserve, relatively new and trying to secure itself with plant-life. Highway 103 north from Ilwaco.

During low tides much of Willapa Bay is an expanse of thick mud flats; fifteen thousand acres of bay are privately owned for the production of oysters. An interesting view of the bay is from Highway 105 west of Raymond.

Highway 101 makes a loop at the southwest tip of Washington, to include the deep-sea fishing port, Ilwaco. South of town is Fort Canby State Park and access to Cape Disappointment and its two-mile jetty. This strip of land is extremely dangerous to seacraft and has earned the local name "Calamity Corner".

South Bend's waterfront is kept busy by its oyster industry and sea-going vessels of many shapes and sizes. Some interesting local sites include the Pacific County Historical Museum (an old drug store with a pressed tin ceiling and plenty of local artifacts) and domed Pacific County Courthouse atop the hill. Follow 101 west of Raymond to South Bend, a community along a bend in the Willapa River.

This old fisherman's church, near the mouth of the Columbia west of the Astoria Bridge, has been restored with elegant simplicity; its stained glass window is the only color in the weathered exterior. Lewis and Clark picnic wayside is beside the church.

In 1899, four and one-half acres of timber from the nearby Grays River forests were logged and milled in order to construct a wharf and buildings for the U. S. Public Health Service at Knappton on the Columbia River. Here, entire ships bringing immigrants into the country were fumigated with sulphur. The quarantine station was in use for fifty-six years, and abandoned in 1955. Three miles northeast of the Astoria Bridge on Highway 401.

A few miles beyond Grays River and Rosburg along Highway 4, East River Road will take you to the small community of Deep River. The Pioneer Church, built in 1898, is just east of town. The road leads through peaceful countryside and dairyland.

Cathlamet is perched above the Columbia, west of Longview on Highway 4. Roads hug the uneven contours of the hillsides; below are waterfront structures to house and dry fishing nets. One of the two remaining Columbia River ferries operates between here and Westport, Oregon; the other crosses between Roosevelt and Arlington.

Skamokawa is approximately thirty miles west of Longview on Highway 4. Referred to locally as "little Venice", the town is built over three creeks which give the appearance of canals, where graceful gillnet fishing boats are moored.

Cedar Creek Grist Mill, built in 1876, is the only remaining structure of its type in the Northwest. Across the bridge from the mill is the Cedar Creek Fishway with picnic tables and paths which lead to the falls. Eight miles east of Woodland on County Road 16 to Grist Mill Road.

At the edge of the Gifford Pinchot National Forest are the varied shapes of a moss-covered lava flow. Further on are the Ape Caves, formed as an upper crust hardened while the molten lava continued to flow beneath. Follow Highway 503 northeast from Woodland, past Lake Merwin and Cougar into the forest. Mt. St. Helens is to the north.

Silver Lake is on Highway 504, six miles east from Castle Rock exit off Interstate 5. For a pleasant interlude on an afternoon's drive, you can rent a rowboat. From the lake you have an excellent view of Mt. St. Helens to the east. You can continue east on the highway to Spirit Lake, named for the spirit of a young hunter in an Indian legend, who drowned while pursuing a phantom elk. And from here, you can continue, on foot, to forest camps and on up to the top of Mt. St. Helens. It's a rigorous climb though, and takes several hours.

Early-morning hours are an exciting time to walk the lands of the Ridgefield Wildlife Refuge and observe the power and grace of Canadian geese in flight or note the disappearance of a nutria beneath a trail of bubbles. North of Vancouver, take exit 14 from Interstate 5 and drive east to Ridgefield. The wildlife refuge is less than a mile south of town.

Lupine is found wherever you go in the Northwest. There are lupine of the sea-shore and of the plateau, sage lands and barren soils; lupine of the valleys, mountain meadows and high Cascades; you'll find them near forest streams, in open woods and along roads. The beauty of the byways is in taking time to look.

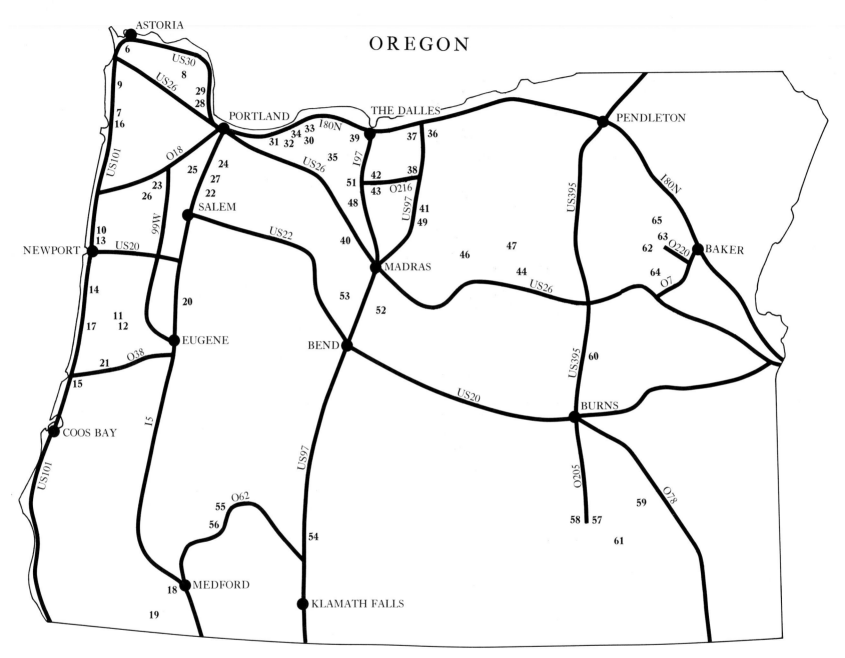

OREGON

Map numbers refer to page numbers. Highway numbers are preceded by letters.

WASHINGTON

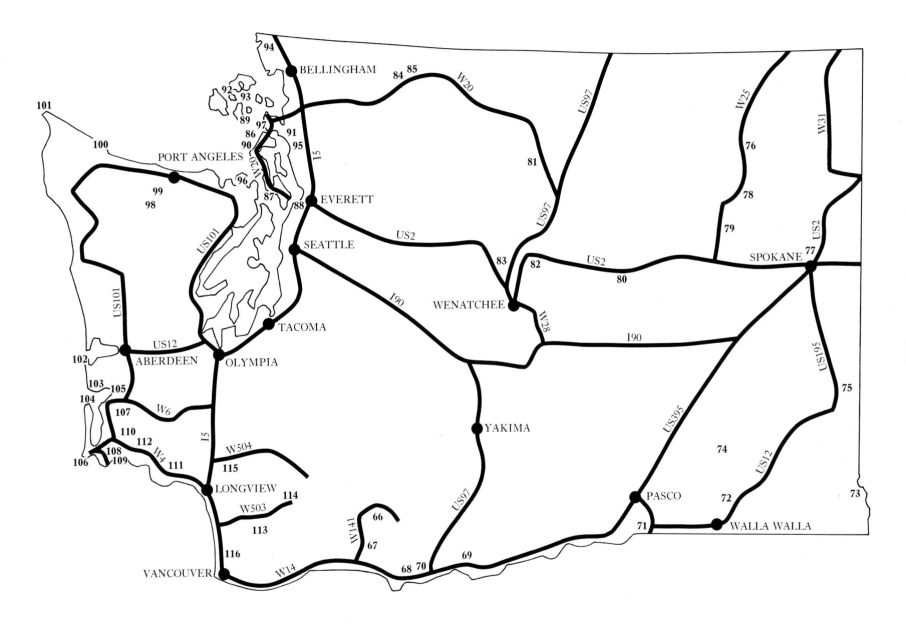